ACROSS THE
USA
ACTIVITY BOOK

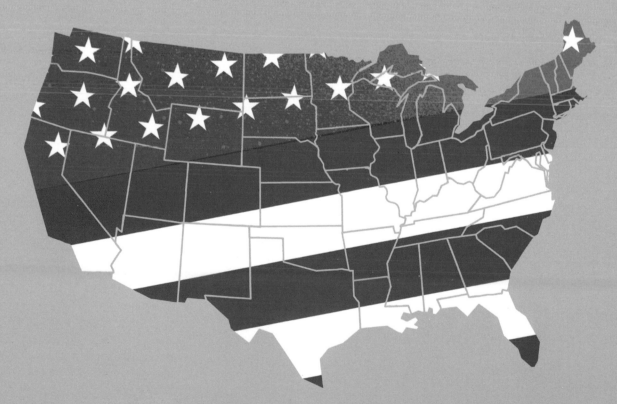

First American Edition 2018
Kane Miller, A Division of EDC Publishing

Text © 2018 Heather Alexander, LLC
Design and layout © 2018 Quarto Publishing plc

For information contact:
Kane Miller, A Division of EDC Publishing
PO Box 470663
Tulsa, OK 74147-0663
www.kanemiller.com
www.edcpub.com
www.usbornebooksandmore.com

Manufactured in Guangdong, China TT112020

ISBN: 978-1-61067-685-4

4 5 6 7 8 9 10

ACROSS THE
USA
ACTIVITY BOOK

HEATHER ALEXANDER

ILLUSTRATED BY MICHAEL MULLAN

Kane Miller
A DIVISION OF EDC PUBLISHING

CONTENTS

USE the MAP

When you see this symbol, turn to the back of the book and use the map to help you complete the activity.

THE 50 STATES

USE the MAP

Here is a map of the United States.
Color the state where you live red.
Color the states you have visited blue.
Color the states you want to visit green.

Capital: Washington, DC

National Bird: Bald Eagle

Add color to the pictures.

National Flower: Rose

Did you know there's a club for people who have visited all 50 states? It's called the All Fifty Club. Write the number of states you have visited here:

....

National Anthem: "The Star-Spangled Banner"

National Mammal: North American Bison

National Tree: Oak

STATE of CONFUSION

Each state has an abbreviation—a shortened version of its name. Check out all 50 abbreviations below.

USE the MAP

MO MISSOURI

GA GEORGIA

AK ALASKA

MI MICHIGAN

OH OHIO

IA IOWA

IN INDIANA

IL ILLINOIS

NM NEW MEXICO

NJ NEW JERSEY

WEST VIRGINIA WV

VA VIRGINIA

PA PENNSYLVANIA

LA LOUISIANA

ARKANSAS AR

MS MISSISSIPPI

WA WASHINGTON

ID IDAHO

DE DELAWARE

VERMONT VT

NV NEVADA

AL ALABAMA

FL FLORIDA

MA MASSACHUSETTS

CA CALIFORNIA

WI WISCONSIN

AZ ARIZONA

CO COLORADO

CT CONNECTICUT

UT UTAH

NE NEBRASKA

SD SOUTH DAKOTA

NY NEW YORK

TX TEXAS

HAWAI'I HI

KS KANSAS

RI RHODE ISLAND

OR OREGON

NH NEW HAMPSHIRE

OK OKLAHOMA

NORTH CAROLINA NC

ME MAINE

KY KENTUCKY

TENNESSEE TN

MARYLAND MD

MINNESOTA MN

MT MONTANA

WY WYOMING

SOUTH CAROLINA SC

ND NORTH DAKOTA

Time for a matching game! First, draw a line from the name of the state to its two-letter abbreviation. Then, draw a line from the abbreviation to the matching state shape.

CALIFORNIA

LOUISIANA

NEW JERSEY

ALASKA

OKLAHOMA

FLORIDA

LA AK OK FL NJ CA

Riddle me a state

STUMP YOUR FRIENDS AND FAMILY WITH THESE WACKY STATE RIDDLES.

1. What are the four newest states?

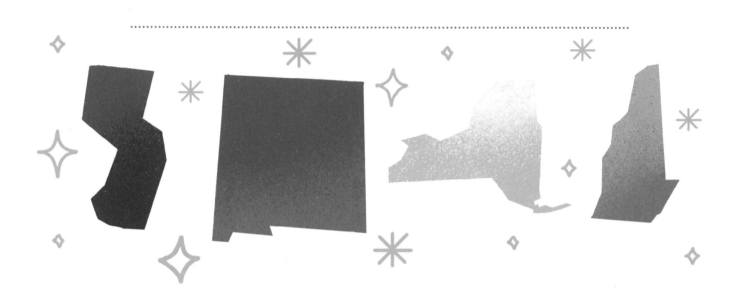

2. What is the smartest state?

3. What is the most colorful state?

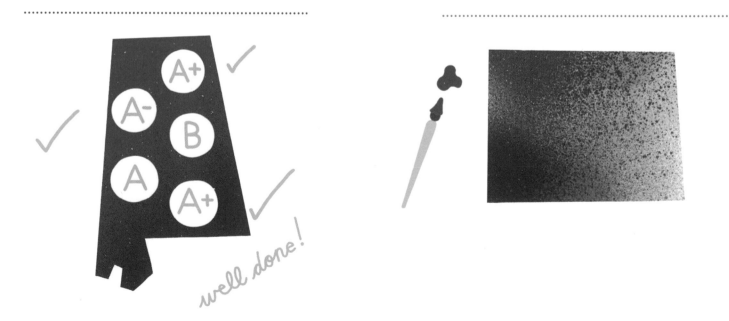

well done!

4. What state do pencils come from?

5. Why does Mississippi see so well?

6. In which state can you find tiny drinks?

7. Which state does the most laundry?

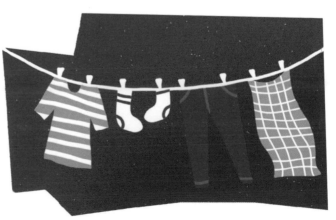

True or False?

Test your knowledge of famous US landmarks and monuments. Check the box—do you think the statement is true or false?

1. The Golden Gate Bridge in San Francisco, California, is painted gold.

TRUE ☐ FALSE ☐

2. Mount Rushmore is in North Dakota.

TRUE ☐ FALSE ☐

3. The Vietnam Veterans Memorial in Washington, DC, was designed by Maya Lin.

TRUE ☐ FALSE ☐

4. Old Faithful in Yellowstone National Park in Wyoming is a geyser that shoots hot chocolate into the air.

TRUE ☐ FALSE ☐

5. The Liberty Bell in Philadelphia, Pennsylvania, is rung every year on the Fourth of July.

TRUE ☐
FALSE ☐

6. Rock found at the bottom of the Grand Canyon in Arizona is close to 2 billion years old.

TRUE ☐ FALSE ☐

7. You can float in the Great Salt Lake in Utah.

TRUE ☐
FALSE ☐

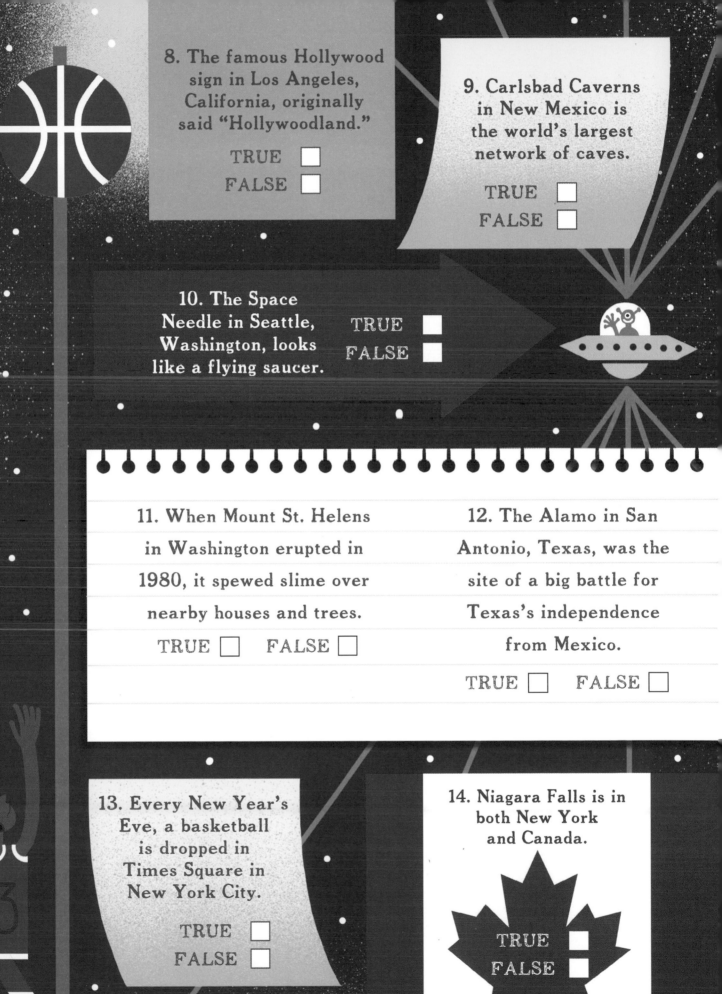

8. The famous Hollywood sign in Los Angeles, California, originally said "Hollywoodland."

TRUE ☐
FALSE ☐

9. Carlsbad Caverns in New Mexico is the world's largest network of caves.

TRUE ☐
FALSE ☐

10. The Space Needle in Seattle, Washington, looks like a flying saucer.

TRUE ☐
FALSE ☐

11. When Mount St. Helens in Washington erupted in 1980, it spewed slime over nearby houses and trees.

TRUE ☐   FALSE ☐

12. The Alamo in San Antonio, Texas, was the site of a big battle for Texas's independence from Mexico.

TRUE ☐   FALSE ☐

13. Every New Year's Eve, a basketball is dropped in Times Square in New York City.

TRUE ☐
FALSE ☐

14. Niagara Falls is in both New York and Canada.

TRUE ☐
FALSE ☐

What's Wrong On The Ranch?

There are many ranches (a type of large farm) in the western United States. Ranchers raise animals such as cattle, sheep and goats. Sometimes they even raise elk, bison or alpacas! Take a close look at this picture of a western ranch, and circle 12 silly things that don't belong.

Super Skyscrapers

Have you ever visited a big city? The biggest cities in the United States have buildings that reach high into the sky. These tall buildings, called skyscrapers, can be more than 40 stories high. Check out these skyscraper facts:

The word "skyscraper" is also an old term for a set of sails on a sailing ship.

Cleaning these huge skyscrapers is a tough job! Window washers are harnessed to a platform at the top of the building. The platform is then lowered downward, so that each window can be cleaned. Would you be brave enough to do it?

Skyscrapers that are over 984 feet are known as "supertall." The US has 17 supertall skyscrapers.

Skyscrapers can actually sway in the wind! Don't worry, though— they are built to stay strong and sturdy, no matter the weather.

Draw your own skyscraper here:

RECORD-BREAKER CODE

Which is the biggest, smallest, highest, deepest? Crack the codes and discover record-breaking places across the United States. Find the coded letter or number on the top row in the tables below. Then write the letter below it in your answer.

Reverse alphabet code

Z	Y	X	W	V	U	T	S	R	Q	P	O	N	M	L	K	J	I	H	G	F	E	D	C	B	A
A	B	C	D	E	F	G	H	I	J	K	L	M	N	O	P	Q	R	S	T	U	V	W	X	Y	Z

Alphabet shift code

Z	A	B	C	D	E	F	G	H	I	J	K	L	M	N	O	P	Q	R	S	T	U	V	W	X	Y
A	B	C	D	E	F	G	H	I	J	K	L	M	N	O	P	Q	R	S	T	U	V	W	X	Y	Z

Number substitution code

1	2	3	4	5	6	7	8	9	10	11	12	13	14	15	16	17	18	19	20	21	22	23	24	25	26
A	B	C	D	E	F	G	H	I	J	K	L	M	N	O	P	Q	R	S	T	U	V	W	X	Y	Z

Use the reverse alphabet code:

1. Which is the largest office building in the United States?

G S V   K V M G Z T L M

_ _ _   _ _ _ _ _ _ _ _

2. Which state is the flattest?

U O L I R W Z

_ _ _ _ _ _ _

3. Which state is the smallest in size?

I S L W V   R H O Z M W

_ _ _ _ _   _ _ _ _ _ _

Use the alphabet shift code:

4. Which state has the fewest people?

V X N L H M F

_ _ _ _ _ _ _

5. Which state has the busiest airport?

F D N Q F H Z

_ _ _ _ _ _ _

6. Which state has the most lighthouses?

L H B G H F Z M

_ _ _ _ _ _ _ _

Use the number substitution code:

7. Crater Lake is the deepest lake in the US. Which state is it in?

15 18 5 7 15 14

_ _ _ _ _ _

8. Denali is the tallest mountain in the US. Which state is it in?

1 12 1 19 11 1

_ _ _ _ _ _

9. Which state has the most caves?

20 5 14 14 5 19 19 5 5

_ _ _ _ _ _ _ _ _

Super Code Breaker! Figure out which code to use.
10. Until 2015, Denali was known by a different name. What was it?

N L F M G   N X P R M O V B

_ _ _ _ _   _ _ _ _ _ _ _

Hint: The mountain was named after a president.

Lady in the Harbor

The Statue of Liberty is an important symbol of the United States. She represents freedom and liberty. The people of France gave her to the US as a gift in 1886. She stands in New York Harbor.

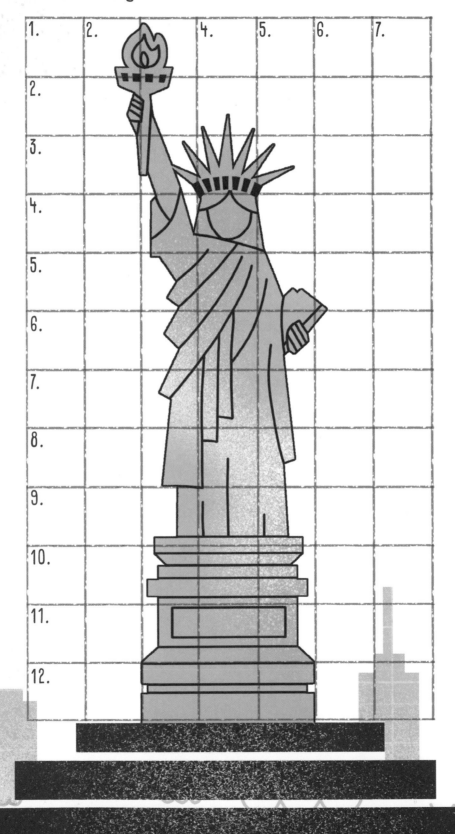

Draw the Statue of Liberty onto the grid below. Copy the picture on the left, square by square, using the numbers as a guide.

1.	2.	3.	4.	5.	6.	7.
2.						
3.						
4.						
5.						
6.						
7.						
8.						
9.						
10.						
11.						
12.						

THE ALL-STAR SEARCH

THE UNITED STATES BOASTS AMAZING ATHLETES IN ALMOST EVERY SPORT. WHAT IS YOUR FAVORITE SPORT? WHO ARE YOUR FAVORITE ATHLETES?

Find the names of these American athletes in the word search. Names may be diagonal, up or down. Some letters may overlap. Circle the names as you find them in the grid, and check them off the list. Once you have found all of the athletes in the word search, link each athlete with their sport.

✓ Simone Biles •	• Tennis
Tom Brady •	• Skiing
Kris Bryant •	• Swimming
Landon Donovan •	• Baseball
Kevin Durant •	• Basketball
Dale Earnhardt Jr. •	• Soccer
LeBron James •	• Swimming
Katie Ledecky •	• Football
Eli Manning •	• Basketball
Alex Morgan •	• Car racing
Nneka Ogwumike •	• Football
Danica Patrick •	• Soccer
Michael Phelps •	• Baseball
Mike Trout •	• Gymnastics
Lindsey Vonn •	• Car racing
Serena Williams •	• Basketball

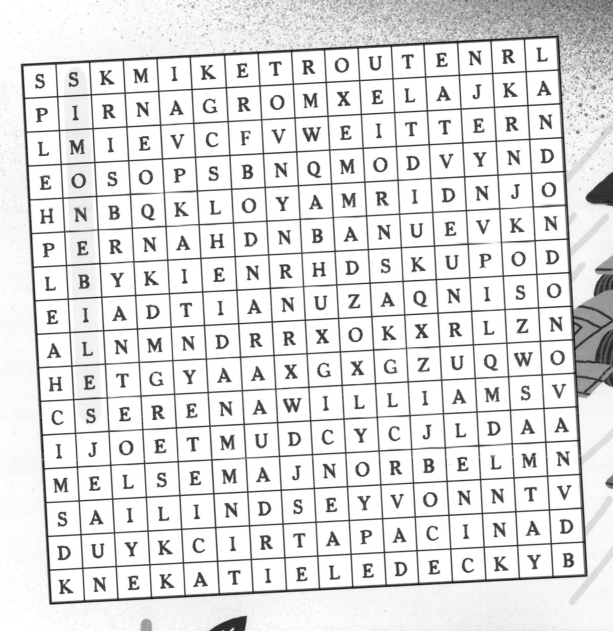

S	S	K	M	I	K	E	T	R	O	U	T	E	N	R	L
P	I	R	N	A	G	R	O	M	X	E	L	A	J	K	A
L	M	I	E	V	C	F	V	W	E	I	T	T	E	R	N
E	O	S	O	P	S	B	N	Q	M	O	D	V	Y	N	D
H	N	B	Q	K	L	O	Y	A	M	R	I	D	N	J	O
P	E	R	N	A	H	D	N	B	A	N	U	E	V	K	N
L	B	Y	K	I	E	N	R	H	D	S	K	U	P	O	D
E	I	A	D	T	I	A	N	U	Z	A	Q	N	I	S	O
A	L	N	M	N	D	R	R	X	O	K	X	R	L	Z	N
H	E	T	G	Y	A	A	X	G	X	G	Z	U	Q	W	O
C	S	E	R	E	N	A	W	I	L	L	I	A	M	S	V
I	J	O	E	T	M	U	D	C	Y	C	J	L	D	A	A
M	E	L	S	E	M	A	J	N	O	R	B	E	L	M	N
S	A	I	L	I	N	D	S	E	Y	V	O	N	N	T	V
D	U	Y	K	C	I	R	T	A	P	A	C	I	N	A	D
K	N	E	K	A	T	I	E	L	E	D	E	C	K	Y	B

WELCOME to My STATE

Your job is to design a fabulous billboard to convince people to visit your state.

WHAT GOES ON A TRAVEL BILLBOARD?

1

Be sure to include the name of your state.

2

Make a list of fun things to do and interesting sights to see in your state.

_____

_____

_____

Now draw them on your billboard. You can use symbols, too.

3

Create a slogan or catchy phrase for your state and add it to your billboard.

Here are some popular travel slogans to spark ideas:

- Wyoming: Forever West
- Texas: It's Like a Whole Other Country
- Connecticut: Still Revolutionary

LICENSE PLATE SCRAMBLE

Highways are filled with cars, trucks and other vehicles—all driving from state to state.

- Major highways are given numbers instead of names. Odd-numbered highways run north and south. Even-numbered highways run east and west.
- Route 20 is the longest highway in the US. It stretches 3,237 miles from Boston, Massachusetts, to Newport, Oregon.

Unscramble the letters on these license plates to find different types of vehicles you might see on the road.

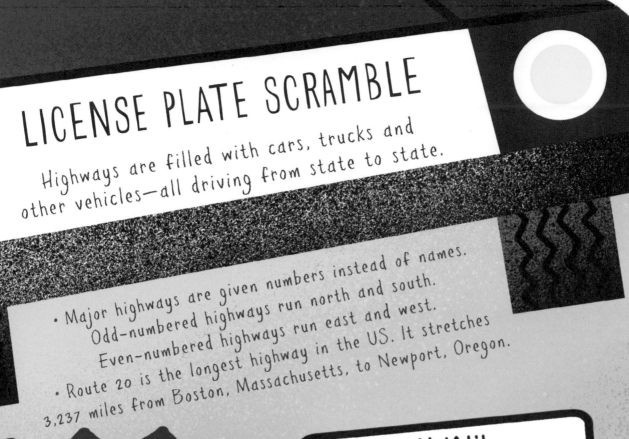

HAWAI'I
XTIA

Vermont
LOSCOH USB
GREEN MOUNTAIN STATE

NEBRASKA
ROTARTC

ALASKA

OCELIP RAC

WEST VIRGINIA

REIF NEGIEN

Scenic IDAHO

CLOTERYMOC

Oregon

EMLUABNCA

California

RUKCT

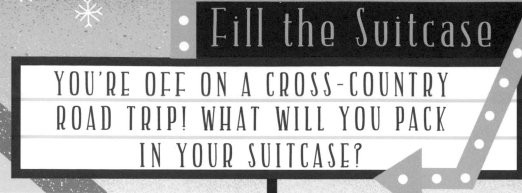

Fill the Suitcase

YOU'RE OFF ON A CROSS-COUNTRY ROAD TRIP! WHAT WILL YOU PACK IN YOUR SUITCASE?

The United States is an enormous country. The weather is different from state to state. Southern states are warmer, while northern states are colder. If you go to Montana in the winter, you'll need snow boots. If you go to Mississippi in the summer, you'll need shorts. If you go to Oregon, you'll need an umbrella. If you go to Arizona, you'll need sunglasses.

Sunniest city: Yuma, Arizona
Hottest states: Florida, Hawai'i, Louisiana
Coldest states: Alaska, North Dakota, Maine
Driest states: Nevada, Utah, Wyoming
Wettest states: Hawai'i, Louisiana, Mississippi
Snowiest city: Rochester, New York
Cloudiest city: Cold Bay, Alaska
Windiest spot: The peak of Mount Washington in New Hampshire

Imagine you're taking a trip to each of the destinations below. What clothing should you take for each trip to stay either warm or cool? List your ideas below. Use the pictures to help you.

Vermont
cold in February

Florida
hot in June

SHOW ME THE MONEY

The US Treasury is changing the design of the $5, $10 and $20 bills. The $20 bill will be redesigned to feature Harriet Tubman. She will be the first black American and the first woman in more than a century to appear on the front of a US bill.

Can you design two pretend $15 bills? Choose two people and draw portraits of them on the front of these bills. Color in your new bills however you want.

15   15

15   15

BASEBALL FIND THE DIFFERENCES

Baseball is one of the most popular sports in the United States. The first US baseball stadium was Forbes Field, built in Pittsburgh, Pennsylvania, in 1909.

There are 12 differences between these two pictures. Can you circle them all?

WHICH *way* OUT?

The US grows more corn than anywhere else in the world! Corn stalks grow so high in the summer and fall that some farmers cut mazes into their cornfields. Can you follow the correct path to reach the end of this corn maze?

START

FINISH

32

FARM SUDOKU

Why do you think the Midwest states (Illinois, Indiana, Iowa, Kansas, Michigan, Minnesota, Missouri, Nebraska, North Dakota, Ohio, South Dakota and Wisconsin) are called the nation's "breadbasket"? It's because they grow so much grain and corn on their farms.

Complete the Sudoku puzzle. Fill each square with one of the following: a tractor, a cow, a barn or a hay bale. Draw the picture or write the word. Each picture or word can appear only once in each row, column and mini-grid.

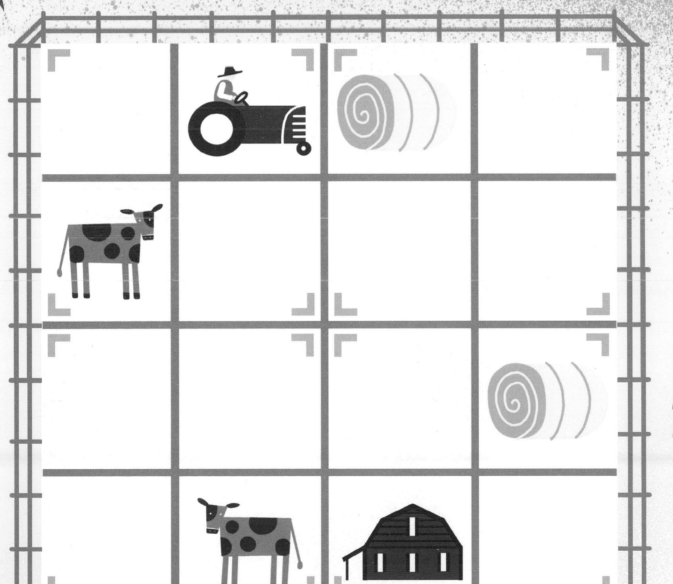

STAR-SPANGLED CELEBRATION

On July 4, 1776, the Declaration of Independence was adopted, granting the thirteen colonies independence from Great Britain. Every year on the Fourth of July, people all over the US celebrate with parades and firework displays.

Study this picture of a Fourth of July parade for two minutes. Then, cover this page with a piece of paper, and from memory, try to answer the questions on page 35. Don't peek back at the picture!

MEMORY TEST

Study the picture on page 34, then answer these questions without looking back at the picture.

1. How many kids were sitting in the wagon?

2. How many balloons was the lady holding?

3. How many US flags were there?

4. How many children were sitting on their parents' shoulders?

5. Is there a dog in the picture?

6. How many people are holding an instrument?

You LIVE Where?

Do you know how your town got its name? Many towns are named after the person who founded it (Carson City, Nevada) or a geographical feature (Rawhide Creek, Nebraska). Some towns have very unusual names. Look at the town signs on these pages and add a drawing to each that matches the town name.

Chicken, ALASKA

Welcome to...
KICKAPOO, *Kansas*

BIG BOTTOM, *Washington*

Monkey Eyebrows, KENTUCKY

TWO EGGS, FLORIDA

Buttzville, New Jersey

Welcome to...
Frankenstein, MISSOURI

Worms, NEBRASKA

ARE WE THERE YET?

HERE IS A FUN GAME TO PLAY ON A ROAD TRIP.

Number of players: 2-6

1. The first player names a real place in the United States. It can be a city, a state, a river, a mountain or a landmark.

2. The second player takes the last letter of the place name and says a place that starts with that letter.

3. The third player takes the last letter of the place name and says a place that starts with that letter.

4. Here's an example: if Player 1 says, "Oregon," Player 2 could say, "New Mexico." Player 3 could say, "Omaha," and so on.

5. A place can't be used twice. If a player can't think of a place, they are out of the game. The winner is the last remaining player.

CAN'T SEE THE FOREST FOR THE TREES

The trees in the Redwood National and State Parks in Northern California are the tallest living things on Earth. They're over 300 feet tall—that's about as tall as the Statue of Liberty! Most redwood trees live to be 500 to 700 years old, but some live as long as 2,000 years.

In this redwood forest, there are two trees that are exactly alike, two owls that are exactly alike and two bears that are exactly alike. Can you find them all?

MY GREAT AMERICAN ROAD TRIP

This game can be played with as many people as you like. Ask your friends and family to say a word that fits the description below each blank space, then write in that word. The sillier the words, the funnier the letter will be! No one should know what the letter says until you have the words needed. When the blanks are filled, read the letter out loud.

Dear ....,
          (Name of friend)

I just got home from the greatest road trip around the United States!

We drove from .... to .... ,
                    (State)   (State)

stopped off in .... and then drove to ....
                    (State)   (State)

Here's what happened: First, we all jumped into the ....
                                                              (Type of car)

I sat in the back with ....
                              (Person you know)

The first thing I spotted out the window was a ....
                                                          (Type of animal)

and it was eating ....
                         (Type of food)

This made us hungry, so we drove to ....
                                                (Name of a restaurant)

and ordered .... with a side of ....
              (Type of food)   (Type of food)

As we drove, we all sang ....
(A song)

The people in the ....
(Type of vehicle)

beside us heard our singing. They held up a sign that said ....
(A message about your singing)

on it. We had been traveling for ....hours,
(Number)

so we stopped to look at the ....
(Famous place)

I snapped a picture. Guess who was behind me in the photo?

A .... that had escaped from the zoo!
(Type of wild animal)

We picked it up and drove it back to the zoo. The zoo said I was a hero!

They gave me 10 pieces of .... ,
(Type of candy)

tickets to see .... and my own ....
(A movie at the theater)   (Type of toy)

Doesn't that sound like a great trip?

Your friend,

....
(Your name)

ROUTE 66

41

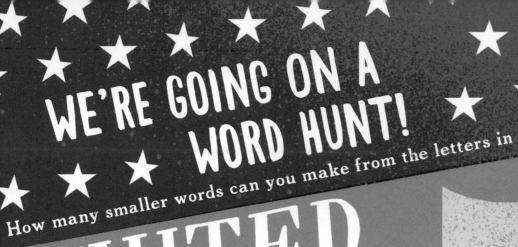

WE'RE GOING ON A WORD HUNT!

How many smaller words can you make from the letters in

UNITED STATES?

All words must be 3 or more letters. Write your answers in the white spaces below.

Keeping score:
Each 3-letter word = 1 point
Each 4-letter word = 2 points
Each 5-letter word = 3 points
Each word with 6 letters or above = 4 points

Add up your total number of points.
YOUR SCORE:

Happy Turkey Day

On the fourth Thursday in November, America celebrates Thanksgiving with food and parades. At the very first Thanksgiving in 1621, the Wampanoag and the first settlers from England ate together. The meal may have included wild turkey, duck, fish, sweet potatoes, cranberries, squash and pumpkin.

Find 12 words associated with Thanksgiving in the word search below.

T	X	X	J	G	Q	Q	R	B	I	L	V	D	M	Y
R	H	S	N	U	A	N	G	L	G	X	J	K	B	Z
Z	Y	U	H	I	E	K	L	Q	Y	X	J	O	Z	U
G	E	I	R	G	K	A	N	O	I	T	A	C	A	V
A	K	Y	L	S	B	P	S	S	G	R	A	V	Y	O
O	R	Q	A	T	D	H	M	T	K	B	O	O	Z	P
N	U	M	O	M	F	A	U	U	A	S	B	S	X	M
A	T	O	B	K	S	F	Y	F	P	M	M	B	P	P
P	F	P	R	A	D	O	K	F	K	S	C	L	L	T
M	R	I	M	Q	A	L	N	I	S	S	Y	Y	E	O
A	E	E	T	Q	I	S	U	N	W	N	M	D	Q	R
W	T	I	V	O	A	D	U	G	P	O	A	F	S	X
Z	Y	Y	B	N	Y	R	E	N	U	R	C	S	I	B
P	I	L	G	R	I	M	S	T	A	L	E	Z	H	O
V	G	A	Z	A	U	S	H	P	I	N	O	R	B	B

Football
Gravy
Parade
Pie

Pilgrims
Plymouth
Pumpkin
Stuffing

Thursday
Turkey
Vacation
Wampanoag

43

IN THE RIGHT DIRECTION

USE the MAP

Do you have a good sense of direction?

The compass to the left shows North, South, East and West. Use the compass and the map of the continental United States (that's the 50 states, not including Alaska and Hawai'i) to answer the questions. Circle your answers.

1. Which state is directly east of Vermont?
   a. New Hampshire
   b. Pennsylvania
   c. Delaware

2. Which state is directly west of Louisiana?
   a. Texas
   b. Alabama
   c. Maine

3. Which state is directly north of Tennessee?
   a. Georgia
   b. Kentucky
   c. Colorado

4. Which state is directly south of Washington?
   a. Iowa
   b. Oregon
   c. Indiana

5. If you wanted to travel from Texas to South Dakota, in which direction would you head?
   a. North
   b. South
   c. East

6. If you wanted to travel from Iowa to Rhode Island, in which direction would you head?
   a. North
   b. South
   c. East

Follow the directions below to find buried treasure hidden in a state. Mark your answer with an X on the map.

7. The treasure is in the state directly south of Minnesota and north of Missouri.

DOWN THE MISSISSIPPI

The Mississippi River flows through ten states: Louisiana, Mississippi, Arkansas, Tennessee, Kentucky, Missouri, Illinois, Iowa, Wisconsin and Minnesota. By moving from rock to rock, can you draw the shortest path across the mighty Mississippi River? You can only use the even-numbered rocks, and you can't go backward.

START

108

7 104 37 29 43

6 62

20 14 80 102

58

15 11 49 33 55 8:

53

22 51 39 9 52 66

34 4 87

16 77 88

47 10 90 35

61 38 96 86 10

25 72 30 7

60

95 73

21

91 13 71

106

78

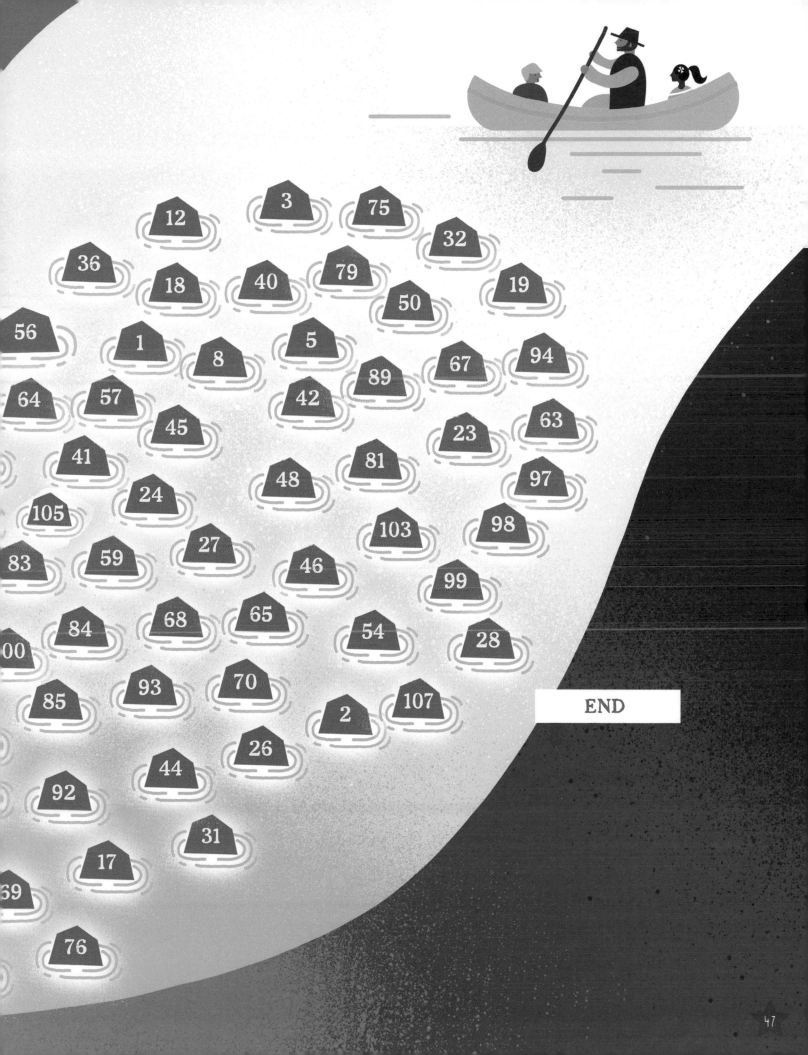

Home Sweet Home

The President of the United States lives and works in the White House. Redecorate the White House below. You could give it a new color or add a pattern—the choice is yours!

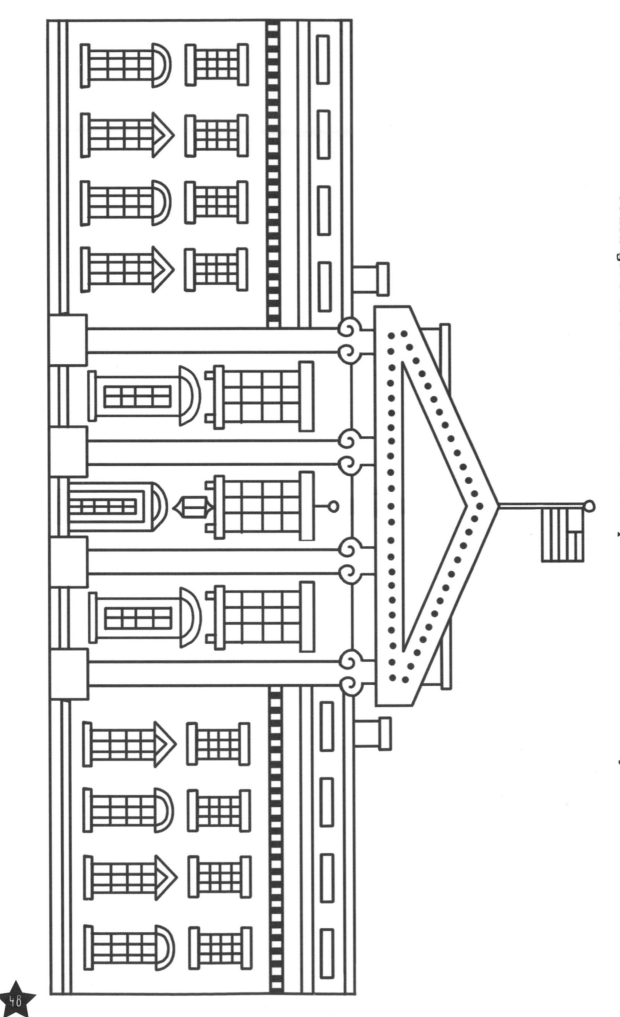

STAR SHINING BRIGHT

The US national anthem is called "The Star-Spangled Banner" because stars are a very important part of the flag. In this jumble of shapes below, there are 3 hidden 5-point stars. Can you color them in?

OVAL OFFICE MAKEOVER

The president works in the Oval Office in the White House. Each president may decorate it any way they like. Some presidents put art on the walls. Some presidents keep the top of their desk clear, while others have piles of papers. One president even kept a jar of jelly beans on his desk!

How would you decorate the Oval Office? Color in the walls and the rug, add artwork to the picture frames and draw what you'd put on your desk.

★ ★ ★ POSTCARD ★ ★ ★
TO THE PRESIDENT

Many different things make the United States great. Write a postcard to the president, saying what you love about the US. Don't forget to sign your name.

Dear Mr. President,

Here's what I love about the US:

....

....

....

....

....

....

TO: The President of
the United States
The White House
1600 Pennsylvania Avenue NW
Washington, DC 20500

STARS and STRIPES FOREVER

Read the facts about the US flag below.
Then, cover the text and answer the
questions on page 53 from memory.

On June 14, 1777, the Continental Congress passed the Flag Act, declaring that a national flag of red, white and blue would be made. Betsy Ross is said to have designed the first flag. The flag's thirteen stripes (seven red and six white) represent the thirteen colonies. The flag has a star for each state. As the colonies became states and new states were added, the number of stars increased. There are now 50 stars—one for each state.

There are a lot of "flag rules." The US flag must be flown at the top of a flagpole, except if someone important has died, when it is flown at half-staff. It is also flown at half-staff from sunrise until noon on Memorial Day. The flag must be taken down at night, unless there is a light shining on it. It must never be flown in bad weather or touch the ground. "Old Glory"—the nickname for the US flag—is celebrated every year on National Flag Day, June 14th.

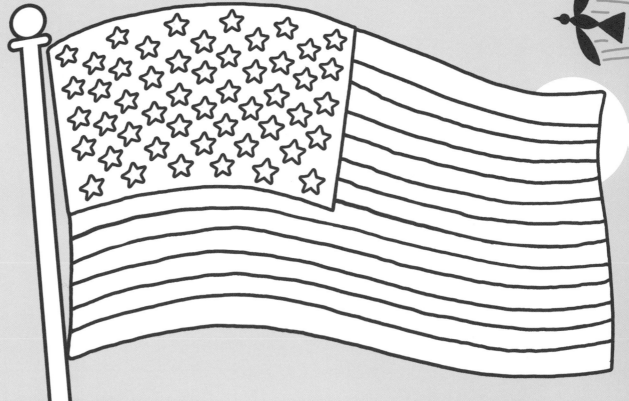

Color the US flag using red and blue.

How much do you remember from
the facts about the flag?

 1. The stars symbolize the number of states. How many stars are on the flag today?

2. The stripes symbolize the original colonies. How many stripes are on the flag?

3. Are there more red stripes or white stripes?

4. Who is said to have designed the first US flag?

5. When is the flag flown at half-staff (halfway up the pole)?

6. The flag can be flown in a thunderstorm. True or false?

7. The flag should never be allowed to touch the ground. True or false?

8. Flag Day is celebrated during what month?

FLY Your FLAG

Every state has its own flag. Here are some of them.

Alabama

Tennessee

Rhode Island

Colorado

Texas

South Carolina

Ohio

Design a flag that represents you. What do you like to do? What people and animals are important to you? Draw them on the flag below, then color it with your favorite colors.

SAY HELLO!

The United States is a country of immigrants. People of different cultures, races and religions have moved here from all over the world, bringing food, customs and languages. That's why the US has been described as a "melting pot." A melting pot is like a big pot of soup—where all the ingredients blend together. English is the most commonly spoken language, but many people in the US speak other languages, too.

How many people do you know who speak another language?

Jeść

mangiare

EAT

ESSEN

COMER

MANGER

"Hello" is written in six different languages below. Draw a line to connect the word "hello" with its language. The food under each word will give you a clue about the culture it comes from.

ITALIAN

HEBREW

CHINESE

SPANISH

GERMAN

JAPANESE

HOLA

CIAO

KONNICHIWA

SHALOM

HALLO

NI HAO

Campfire Conundrum

For hundreds of years, American families and friends have spent time in the wilderness. They sleep under the stars in sleeping bags or tents. They gather around campfires, cooking food, telling stories and singing songs. Have you ever been camping?

In this bag there are:

10 pink marshmallows
10 white marshmallows

yum!

MARSHMALLOWS

Around the fire there are:
- 2 sets of double pink marshmallow sticks
- 3 sets of mixed (1 white, 1 pink) double marshmallow sticks
- 3 sets of single white marshmallow sticks.

Color the pink marshmallows, then write your answer to the following question in the box.

How many pink marshmallows are left in the bag?

GOING SHOPPING

Travel through the maze from start to finish and pick up the foods on the shopping list. You need to find the six foods in the order in which they are listed. Good luck!

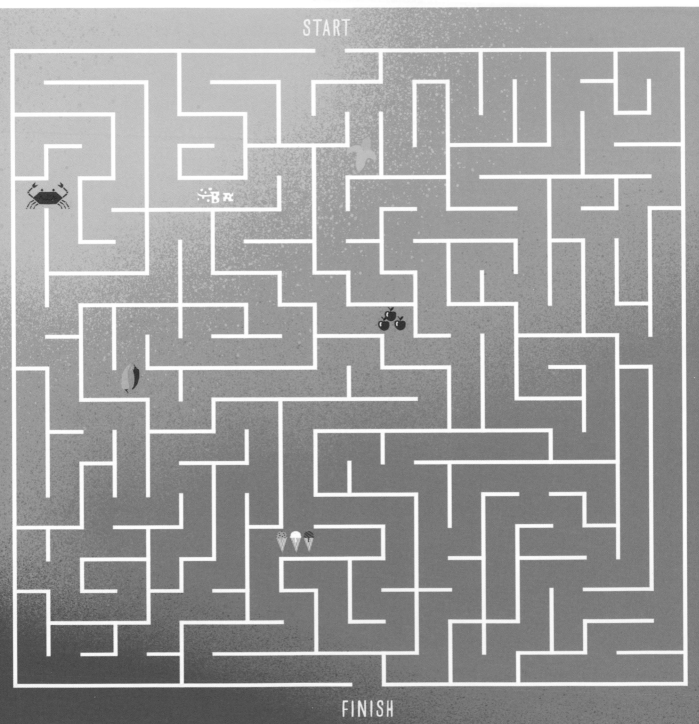

START

FINISH

SHOPPING LIST

1. Iowa corn
2. Washington apples
3. Wisconsin cheddar
4. Maryland crabs
5. New Mexico chili peppers
6. Vermont ice cream

UNITED SWEETS OF AMERICA

Find the yummy desserts listed below in this word search. Words may be forward, diagonal, up or down. Some letters may overlap. Circle the words as you find them and cross them off the list. You only need to find the name of each dessert, not the name of the state. The words in the grid don't include spaces or punctuation.

```
      S H O O F L Y P I E D I
      Y O T N T D R B S N D C N P
    S N I C K E R D O O D L E B A H
    V Q Z J B S H S W S O U R B U U B M
  J G F E H H C J A C T W G K B C E L A M
F P H D W T X G W L E O W O I K K S I R N S
U M I F E V S Y C T U N H O L N E U T I I H
D I R T C A K E A W Y C U E O O Y G R O Y A
G I K N H J S G K A H R B Y I P E A Y N J V
E N L W E C D V Z T T E H B U J C R M B M E
N J E Q E E B B X E R A N U J B A C N E K I
B D H B S B P D R R R M R T L O N R P R L C
J I C N E H H I Y T A P J T U P D E S R I E
O N Q H C J P P A A S I B E Z C Y A M Y O M
W A Y N A U I T N F M E M R K X B M O P Y N
  E C N K E Y B A F R Q Q C A S D P R I O
  Y B E V Y D F Y E A M A T A L I E E
    Y N L J U T P L J N K V C N E S
      I R N D I P Q B M E U Y N L
      K E Y L I M E P I E A W
```

Marionberry pie (Oregon)
Saltwater taffy (New Jersey)
Shave ice (Hawai'i)
Shoo-fly pie (Pennsylvania)
S'mores (Vermont)
Snickerdoodle (Connecticut)
Sugar cream pie (Indiana)

Boston cream pie (Massachusetts)
Buckeye candy (Ohio)
Cheesecake (New York)
Dirt cake (Kansas)
Fudge (Michigan)
Gooey butter cake (Missouri)
Huckleberry pie (Idaho)
Key lime pie (Florida)

PACK A PICNIC

You're going on a picnic. Study the foods from different states on page 63, then draw your favorites on the plates.

- Corned beef sandwich, Ohio
- Chicken-fried steak, Oklahoma
- Blueberry muffin, Minnesota
- Pulled pork, North Carolina
- Shrimp and grits, South Carolina
- Pepperoni roll, West Virginia
- Cornbread, Alabama
- Salmon, Alaska
- Pink tomatoes, Arkansas
- Hamburgers, Connecticut
- Peaches, Georgia
- Pineapple, Hawai'i
- Deep-dish pizza, Illinois
- Popcorn, Indiana
- Barbecue ribs, Kansas
- Fried chicken, Kentucky
- Gumbo, Louisiana
- Crab cakes, Maryland
- Lobster, Maine
- Cherries, Michigan
- Steak, Nevada
- Bagels, New York
- Fried pickles, Tennessee
- Beef jerky, Wyoming

DID I WAKE YOU?

USE the MAP

YOU'RE EATING BREAKFAST AT 8:00 A.M. IN VERMONT AND YOU CALL YOUR FRIEND IN OREGON. HE DOESN'T ANSWER. WHY NOT? HE'S FAST ASLEEP. IT'S 5:00 A.M. IN OREGON! WHY IS THE TIME DIFFERENT?

The continental United States is divided into four time zones. This way, each region has the same balance of daylight and darkness. The four time zones are: Eastern, Central, Mountain and Pacific. Each zone is 1 hour different from the one beside it.

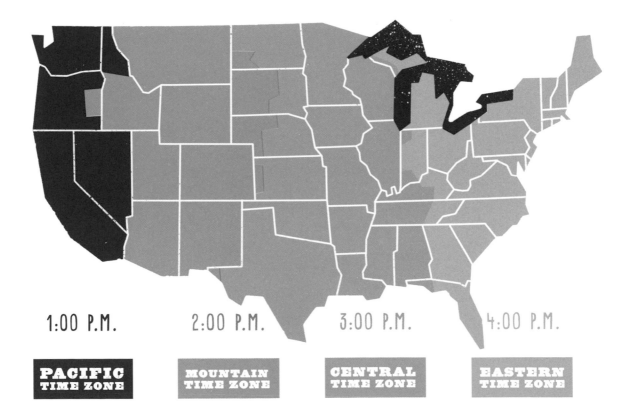

1:00 P.M.   2:00 P.M.   3:00 P.M.   4:00 P.M.

PACIFIC TIME ZONE   **MOUNTAIN TIME ZONE**   **CENTRAL TIME ZONE**   **EASTERN TIME ZONE**

So, when it's 4:00 p.m. Eastern time, it's 3:00 p.m. Central time, 2:00 p.m. Mountain time and 1:00 p.m. Pacific time.

READ THE QUESTIONS, THEN DRAW THE HANDS OF THE CLOCKS TO SHOW THE CORRECT TIMES.

1. If Juan wakes up at 9:00 a.m. in South Carolina and texts Uncle Eric in Arkansas, what time is it for Uncle Eric?

2. Kayla and Karlie are both jumping rope. Kayla is in Louisiana and Karlie is in Wyoming. It's 2:00 p.m. for Kayla. What time is it for Karlie?

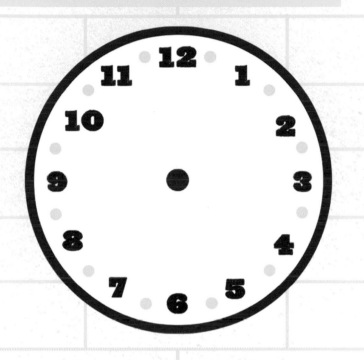

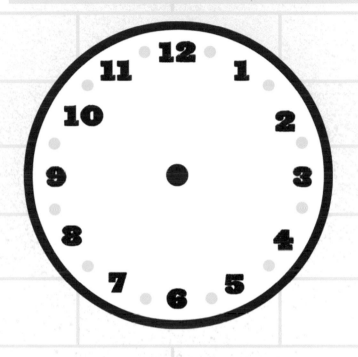

3. Meiko is eating dinner in California, while Saria is asleep in Rhode Island. If it is 6:00 p.m. for Meiko, what time is it for Saria?

4. Nick ice-skates in Wisconsin, while Aiden builds a snowman in Montana. If it's 3:00 p.m. for Nick, what time is it for Aiden?

FLOWER POWER

EVERY STATE HAS AN OFFICIAL FLOWER. IN EACH ROW,
CIRCLE THE ONE FLOWER THAT IS DIFFERENT FROM THE REST.

Violet, Illinois
Fact: Violets contain
a lot of vitamin C.

Sunflower, Kansas
Fact: Each sunflower has as
many as 1,000 to 2,000 seeds.

Red Carnation, Ohio
Fact: Ohio honors President William
McKinley with this flower. He often
wore a red carnation on his lapel.

Bitterroot, Montana
Fact: Bitterroot can live up
to a year without water.

Sego Lily, Utah
Fact: Early settlers ate the root
of the sego lily when they didn't
have any other food.

ROCKY MOUNTAIN RACE

The tall Rocky Mountains, also called "The Rockies," are in the western United States. These snowboarders are racing down the Rockies. Follow the lines to find out which snowboarder makes it all the way down the mountain and wins the race.

STATE DOODLES

Give these states arms, legs, hair, glasses
or even a mustache. One has been done for you.

CALIFORNIA

GEORGIA

MONTANA

ILLINOIS

WISCONSIN

SOUTH CAROLINA

TEXAS

NEW YORK

WACKY & WEIRD

The United States has some crazy laws!
Read the twelve US laws on these pages.
Can you find and circle the three
that are fake?

It's illegal to
wake a sleeping
bear to take a
photo in Alaska.

It's illegal to have
exploding golf balls
in Massachusetts.

It's illegal to dance
with a coyote in
New Mexico.

It's illegal to drive a
camel on the highway
in Nevada.

It's illegal to
whistle underwater
in West Virginia.

It's illegal to have an elephant plow a cotton field in North Carolina.

It's illegal to keep a horse in a bathtub in South Carolina.

It's illegal to wear gloves on your feet in Hawai'i.

It's illegal to eat soup with a fork in New York.

It's illegal to do a backflip on Thursdays in New Hampshire.

It's illegal to keep an ice cream cone in your back pocket on Sundays in Georgia.

It's illegal to cross state lines with a duck on top of your head in Minnesota.

GOLD RUSH!

This is Bea.

Last night, she struck it rich.
She collected 14 bags of gold.

The bank was closed, so she hid the bags around the mining town. This morning, Bea can't remember where she hid them. Can you help her find her 14 bags of gold?

HOTEL

BANK

Ticket to Ride

Unscramble the destination board at the bus station to discover which US city each bus is traveling to. Use the clues to help you.

11:51

→ **LADORNO**

_____
Home of Disney World

→ **NAS TONIONA**

_____
Home of the Alamo

→ **OCCIGHA**

_____
Home of The Willis Tower

→ **HIPHEDALIAPL**

_____
Home of the Liberty Bell

DEPARTURES

11:51

→ **ENW SNOLAER**

....
Home of the Mardi Gras parade

→ **NINOLISAMEP**

....
One of the Twin Cities

→ **ALEEHN**

....
Capital of Montana

→ **VASHLINEL**

- - - - - - - - - - - - - - - - - - - -
Capital of Tennessee

WHO AM I?

Read the descriptions of these famous Americans, then write their names in the spaces provided. Use the word bank if you need a clue.

I refused to sit at the back of the bus. I helped start a boycott of the buses in Montgomery, Alabama. I fought to end racial segregation.
Who am I?

I was an astronaut. I rode the Apollo 11 spacecraft that launched from the Kennedy Space Center in Florida. On July 21, 1969, I was the first man to walk on the moon.
Who am I?

My research lab was in Menlo Park, New Jersey. I invented the phonograph. I also invented the first light bulb that could be used in the home.
Who am I?

WORD BANK:

Harriet Tubman   Rosa Parks   Neil Armstrong
Thomas Alva Edison   Susan B. Anthony   Benjamin Franklin
George Washington

I flew a kite in a thunderstorm to prove that lightning is fast electricity. I am one of the Founding Fathers of the United States. I lived in Philadelphia, Pennsylvania.
Who am I?

I was the commander of the Continental Army. I was the first President. I lived in Mount Vernon, Virginia.
Who am I?

I started the National Women's Suffrage Association in 1869 with Elizabeth Cady Stanton. I helped women get the right to vote in the United States. I am on the dollar coin.
Who am I?

I was born into slavery on a plantation in Maryland. I escaped to Pennsylvania using the Underground Railroad. I bravely led 300 other slaves to freedom.
Who am I?

Send a Postcard

THESE POSTCARDS ARE EACH FROM A DIFFERENT STATE. DRAW A PICTURE
ON EACH POSTCARD—YOU COULD DRAW A FAMOUS PERSON FROM THERE,
A FAMOUS MONUMENT OR A PLACE OF NATURAL BEAUTY.

ARKANSAS

MINNESOTA

VERMONT

WASHINGTON

Derby Day

THE KENTUCKY DERBY IS A HORSE RACE HELD EVERY YEAR ON THE FIRST SATURDAY IN MAY, IN LOUISVILLE, KENTUCKY. THE RACE IS 1.25 MILES LONG, AND THE HORSES RUNNING MUST BE THREE-YEAR-OLDS. SINCE 1875, THE DERBY HAS BEEN CALLED "THE MOST EXCITING TWO MINUTES IN SPORTS."

Find and circle 10 items in the audience at the Kentucky Derby that start with the letter H.

BALLOON FIESTA

Up, up and away! Every year there's an enormous hot-air balloon festival in Albuquerque, New Mexico. The sky fills with brilliant color as hundreds of giant balloons take flight. Color in your own hot-air balloon below.

THE TOP FIVE

Check out these Top-5 Lists for everything United States.

The Tallest Roller Coasters

1. Kingda Ka (New Jersey)
2. Top Thrill Dragster (Ohio)
3. Superman: Escape From Krypton (California)
4. Fury 325 (North Carolina)
5. Millennium Force (Ohio)

The Smallest States (by land area)

1. Rhode Island
2. Delaware
3. Connecticut
4. Hawai'i
5. New Jersey

The Most Popular Ice Cream Flavors

1. Vanilla
2. Chocolate
3. Cookies & cream
4. Mint chocolate chip
5. Chocolate chip cookie dough

The Most Popular Pizza Toppings

1. Pepperoni
2. Mushrooms
3. Onions
4. Sausage
5. Bacon

Now, write your own Top-5 lists!

My Favorite States

1. ....
2. ....
3. ....
4. ....
5. ....

My Favorite Animals

1. ....
2. ....
3. ....
4. ....
5. ....

My Favorite Playgrounds

1. ....
2. ....
3. ....
4. ....
5. ....

My Favorite Books

1. ....
2. ....
3. ....
4. ....
5. ....

My Favorite Colors

1. ....
2. ....
3. ....
4. ....
5. ....

SAY WHAT?

What would these famous monuments and statues say if they could speak? Fill in the speech bubbles—the funnier, the better.

Mount Rushmore is carved into the Black Hills of South Dakota. The sculpture shows the faces of George Washington, Thomas Jefferson, Theodore Roosevelt and Abraham Lincoln.

The Golden Driller is in Tulsa, Oklahoma. Tulsa used to be famous for oil drilling.

Lucy the Elephant is the world's largest elephant statue. She stands six stories high in Margate City, New Jersey.

Salem Sue in New Salem, North Dakota, is the world's biggest fiberglass cow. She's 38 feet tall and 50 feet long. She stands on a hill, so you can even spot her from places that are two hours away!

If you could erect a statue in your hometown, what would it look like? Draw your statue here and give it a name.

BEYOND THE USA

In 1969, the United States became the first country to land a spacecraft on the Moon. Astronauts planted the US flag on the Moon's surface. Use the code in the asteroid shower to figure out the answers to the questions below.

| 1 T | 3 I | 12 C | 11 M | 23 N | 18 G | 20 B | 8 Q | 16 D | 6 F | 7 R | 13 P | 14 E | 22 A | 24 W | 26 H | 5 L | 15 V | 21 Y | 25 K | 17 O | 9 U | 4 J | 10 S | 19 Z | 2 X |

1. Who was the second person to walk on the Moon?

20 9 19 19   22 5 16 7 3 23

_ _ _ _   _ _ _ _ _ _

2. Which state was he from?

23 14 24   4 14 7 10 14 21

_ _ _ _ _ _ _ _ _

3. Where is NASA's headquarters?

24 22 10 26 3 23 18 1 17 23 16 12

_ _ _ _ _ _ _ _ _ _ _ _

Astronauts stitch mission patches onto their spacesuits. These patches have symbols that represent the missions they have been on. If you went to the Moon, what would your mission patch look like? Design your patch below.

Would you travel to outer space? Draw yourself in the astronaut portrait below.

BONES IN THE BACKYARD

DINOSAURS ROAMED THE EARTH 230 TO 65 MILLION YEARS AGO. EVEN THOUGH THE DINOSAURS HAVE ALL DIED OUT, THEIR FOSSILIZED BONES ARE STILL BEING FOUND. LOTS OF DINOSAUR SKELETONS HAVE BEEN DISCOVERED ACROSS THE UNITED STATES.

Triceratops skeleton, discovered in Colorado.

Tyrannosaurus rex skeleton, discovered in South Dakota.

Diplodocus skeleton, discovered in Wyoming.

In 2015, a four-year-old boy found the bone of a 100-million-year-old dinosaur while digging in Mansfield, Texas. What if you discovered a dinosaur buried in your backyard? What would it look like? Draw your dinosaur in the space below.

KNACK FOR NICKNAMES

EACH STATE HAS A NICKNAME. COMPLETE THE CROSSWORD WITH THE NAME OF EACH STATE. READ THE INFORMATION ON PAGE 91 AND USE THE STATE SHAPES AS A CLUE.

USE the MAP

Across
1. The Beehive State
5. The Golden State
7. The Beaver State
9. The Land of Enchantment
10. The Show-Me State

Down
2. The Volunteer State
3. The Pine Tree State
4. The Hoosier State
6. The Equality State
8. The Lone Star State

Add color to the pictures.

• The Golden State was named for the gold discovered here in 1848.

• The Hoosier State is a mystery—no one knows how it got its nickname.

• The Show-Me State's nickname honors the common sense of its people.

• The Land of Enchantment describes this state's scenic beauty.

• The Beaver State is named after its state animal.

• The Beehive State got its name from the beehive, a symbol representing strength in community and determination.

• The Equality State was the first state to elect a female governor and the first state to pioneer the right of women to vote.

• The Pine Tree State is filled with pine tree forests.

• The Volunteer State honors its residents' willingness to volunteer for service.

• The Lone Star State has a single, white, five-pointed star on its state flag.

THE NATION'S CAPITAL

Washington, DC, the District of Columbia, is the capital of the United States. It is located between Virginia and Maryland, on the north bank of the Potomac River. It is not one of the 50 states, because the Constitution doesn't allow the nation's capital to be a state. This is to make sure that no state can become more powerful than the others simply because it houses the capital.

Washington, DC, is home to many important government buildings, monuments, memorials and museums. Can you circle the four buildings that are *not* found in Washington, DC?

WASHINGTON MONUMENT

US CAPITOL

THE SUPREME COURT

THE GIZA PYRAMIDS

BIG BEN

TAJ MAHAL

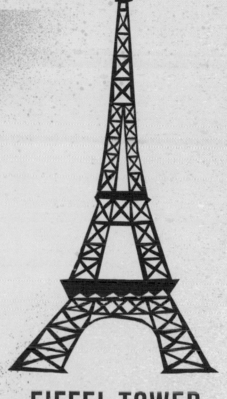

EIFFEL TOWER

LINCOLN MEMORIAL

THE WHITE HOUSE

THOMAS JEFFERSON MEMORIAL

HIDE-AND-SEEK

Cross out the Xs, Ys and Zs to find the state hidden within each group of letters. We've done the first one for you.

~~XY~~W~~Z~~IS~~ZXC~~Y~~~O~~N~~YZSXIX~~N

WISCONSIN

1. MXYIYNZNZXEYXSOYTAZ

_____

2. IDZXAXZHOYX

_____

3. ZYXVZYEXRZMYXONZYT

_____

4. YGEXZORGYXZXIXYA

_____

5. XARXKYANZXSXYAS

_____

BALD EAGLE

The bald eagle is the national bird of the United States.

Finish drawing the feathers on this bald eagle, then color them in.

A bald eagle isn't really bald. Its head is covered with white feathers.

It uses its talons (sharp claws on its feet) to capture prey.

It is at the top of the food chain and has no natural predators.

It can fly as high as 10,000 feet.

The largest bald eagles live in Alaska.

CRAZY CONTESTS

There are many contests and festivals held throughout the United States. Four contests or festivals are written on each trophy below. Three are real, but one is fake. Can you find and circle the fake contest or festival on each trophy?

1. Food, Glorious Food

BARBECUE FESTIVAL
Lexington, North Carolina

MARSHMALLOW MASH-UP
North Chill, Minnesota

CEREALFEST
Battle Creek, Michigan

ROADKILL COOK-OFF
Marlinton, West Virginia

2. Creepy-Crawlies

THE STINK BUG SMELL-EBRATION
Aroma, Delaware

THE GREAT TEXAS
MOSQUITO FESTIVAL
Clute, Texas

TARANTULA AWARENESS
FESTIVAL
Coarsegold, California

TEXAS BUTTERFLY
FESTIVAL
Mission, Texas

3. Make Some Noise

CHICKEN CLUCKING CONTEST
Baltimore, Maryland

YODEL-OFF!
Cacophony, Colorado

LOWER KEYS UNDERWATER
MUSIC FESTIVAL
Ramrod Key, Florida

COTATI ACCORDION
FESTIVAL
Cotati, California

4. Going to Extremes

POLAR BEAR PLUNGE
Point Pleasant, New Jersey

GREAT BATHTUB RACE
Nome, Alaska

JALEPEÑO EATING CONTEST
Laredo, Texas

FLAME JUGGLING FEST
Char, Oklahoma

5. Gross!

ROTTEN SNEAKER CONTEST
Montpelier, Vermont

PIG FEET EATING CONTEST
Swineville, Ohio

**WISCONSIN STATE COW CHIP
THROW AND FESTIVAL**
Prairie du Sac, Wisconsin

FROZEN DEAD GUYS DAY
Nederland, Colorado

6. Grown in the Ground

HUMONGOUS FUNGUS FEST
Crystal Falls, Michigan

NATIONAL LENTIL FESTIVAL
Pullman, Washington

GILROY GARLIC FESTIVAL
Gilroy, California

RADISH EATING CONTEST
Crimson, New Mexico

You just won a blue ribbon at the state fair.
Follow the directions and draw a line from
start to finish to claim your prize.

START

Begin at the START sign.
Follow the path around the bend
until you see the WHITE COW in front
of the CORN STAND. Follow the path
between the WHITE COW and the
FAIRGROUND RIDE. Go straight until you
see the HOT DOG TRUCK. From there,
travel down past the LADY WITH THE PINK
BALLOON toward the SHEEP PEN. Keep
going past the YELLOW AND BLUE COWS
until you reach the ICE CREAM STAND.
You will see the BLUE RIBBON TENT
up ahead!

CORN

SNACKS

ICE CREAM

yum !!!

FINISH

93

DETECTIVE NEEDED

USE the MAP

Kesha, Laurel, Marco and Derek each visited a different state on vacation and took a different pet with them. Your job is to figure out who went where and which pet they took. Make an "X" in each box when you have figured out each clue—one is already done for you.

1. Derek crossed the Golden Gate Bridge.

2. Marco brought his four-legged pet to Detroit.

3. Kesha swam in the Atlantic Ocean. Her pet wears shoes.

4. Laurel visited the Grand Canyon. Her pet eats seeds.

	STATES					PETS			
	Arizona	Florida	Michigan	California		Horse	Fish	Bird	Dog
Kesha									
Laurel	X								
Marco									
Derek									

FOOTBALL CRISSCROSS

Did you know that football is the most popular sport in the US? (Baseball comes in second.) Fans love football's fast-paced excitement. While many enjoy playing the sport, most football fans sit in the bleachers or around a television set to cheer on their favorite team.

Fill in the crisscross grid, using the football words below.

4 letters BALL GOAL	**6 letters** HELMET	**7 letters** BIG GAME DEFENSE OFFENSE
8 letters FULLBACK	**9 letters** TOUCHDOWN	**10 letters** LINEBACKER **11 letters** QUARTERBACK

THE DAY THE ALIEN LANDED

What if an alien from outer space visited the United States? What would it do and where would it go? Write a short story about what would happen. Try to include some of the words from the word bank. Remember to describe what the alien looks like, what it wants and where it has traveled from.

ME

Now that your journey across the 50 states is nearly over, fill in these scrapbook pages to help you record things you love about the United States.

MY HOUSE

MY STATE

MY FAVORITE AMERICAN

MY FAVORITE PLACE IN THE US

ANSWERS

PAGES 8-9: STATE OF CONFUSION

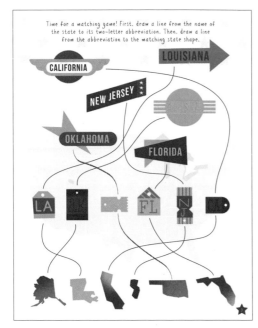

PAGES 10-11: RIDDLE ME A STATE

1. *New* Jersey, *New* Mexico, *New* York and *New* Hampshire.
2. Alabama (it is spelled with four As and one B).
3. Colorado (*color*-ado)
4. Pennsylvania (*pencil*-vania)
5. Mississippi is spelled with four Is (four eyes).
6. Minnesota (mini-*soda*)
7. *Washing*ton

PAGES 12-13: TRUE OR FALSE?

1. False. It is painted "International Orange."
2. False. Mount Rushmore is in South Dakota.
3. True.
4. False. Old Faithful shoots hot water into the air, every 60 to 90 minutes.
5. False. The Liberty Bell hasn't been rung since 1846. Every year on the Fourth of July, it is tapped thirteen times—once for each of the original colonies. It is also tapped on Martin Luther King Jr. Day.
6. True.
7. True. The water in the Great Salt Lake is four times saltier than ocean water, so it's great for floating.
8. True.
9. True.
10. True.

11. False. Mount St. Helens is a volcano. Lava and ash came out when it erupted—not slime.
12. True. Texas was part of Mexico until 1836. It became a state in 1845.
13. False. A lighted crystal ball drops as the current year ends and the new year begins. It takes 60 seconds for the ball to fall.
14. True.

PAGES 14-15: WHAT'S WRONG ON THE RANCH?

PAGES 18-19: RECORD-BREAKER CODE

Reverse alphabet code:
1. The Pentagon
2. Florida
3. Rhode Island

Alphabet shift code:
4. Wyoming
5. Georgia
6. Michigan

Number substitution code:
7. Oregon
8. Alaska
9. Tennessee

Super Code Breaker!
10. Mount McKinley
Use the reverse alphabet code to unlock the answer.

PAGES 22-23: THE ALL-STAR SEARCH

Simone Biles: Gymnastics
Tom Brady: Football
Kris Bryant: Baseball
Landon Donovan: Soccer
Kevin Durant: Basketball
Dale Earnhardt Jr.: Car racing
LeBron James: Basketball
Katie Ledecky: Swimming
Eli Manning: Football
Alex Morgan: Soccer
Nneka Ogwumike: Basketball
Danica Patrick: Car racing
Michael Phelps: Swimming
Mike Trout: Baseball
Lindsey Vonn: Skiing
Serena Williams: Tennis

S	S	K	M	I	K	E	T	R	O	U	T	E	N	R	L
P	I	R	N	A	G	R	O	M	X	E	L	A	J	K	A
L	M	I	E	V	C	F	V	W	E	I	T	T	E	R	N
E	O	S	O	P	S	B	N	Q	M	O	D	V	Y	N	D
H	N	B	Q	K	L	O	Y	A	M	R	I	D	N	J	O
P	E	R	N	A	H	D	N	B	A	N	U	E	V	K	N
L	B	Y	K	I	E	N	R	H	D	S	K	U	P	O	D
E	I	A	D	T	I	A	N	U	Z	A	Q	N	I	S	O
A	L	N	M	N	D	R	R	X	O	K	X	R	L	Z	N
H	E	T	G	Y	A	A	X	G	X	G	Z	U	Q	W	O
C	S	E	R	E	N	A	W	I	L	L	I	A	M	S	V
I	J	O	E	T	M	U	D	C	Y	C	J	L	D	A	A
M	E	L	S	E	M	A	J	N	O	R	B	E	L	M	N
S	A	I	L	I	N	D	S	E	Y	V	O	N	N	T	V
D	U	Y	K	C	I	R	T	A	P	A	C	I	N	A	D
K	N	E	K	A	T	I	E	L	E	D	E	C	K	Y	B

PAGES 26-27: LICENSE PLATE SCRAMBLE

XTIA = TAXI
LOSCOH USB = SCHOOL BUS
ROTARTC = TRACTOR
REIF NEGIEN = FIRE ENGINE
OCELIP RAC = POLICE CAR
CLOTERYMOC = MOTORCYCLE
EMLUABNCA = AMBULANCE
RUKCT = TRUCK

PAGE 31: BASEBALL FIND THE DIFFERENCES

PAGE 32: WHICH WAY OUT?

PAGE 33: FARM SUDOKU

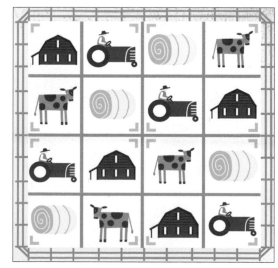

PAGES 34–35: STAR-SPANGLED CELEBRATION

1. 2
2. 3
3. 5
4. 3
5. No
6. 5

PAGE 39: CAN'T SEE THE FOREST FOR THE TREES

PAGE 42: WE'RE GOING ON A WORD HUNT!

Here are some of the words you can make
(not including plurals):

3 letters: aid, and, ant, ate, eat, end, den, die, net,
nut, sea, see, set, sit, sun, tea, ten, tie, tin

4 letters: aunt, date, dean, dent, diet, dine, duet, dune,
dust, east, edit, need, nest, nude, said, sane, seat,
seed, seen, sent, side, site, suit, test, tied, tide, tint,
tune, unit

5 letters: attend, diner, satin, suite, stint, taste,
tease, untie, unite

6 letters: estate, statue, sunset, tinted

7 letters: dentist, stained, stunted, tainted

PAGE 43: HAPPY TURKEY DAY

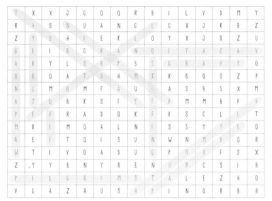

PAGES 44–45: IN THE RIGHT DIRECTION

1. a
2. a
3. b
4. b
5. a
6. c
7. The buried treasure is in Iowa.

PAGES 46–47: DOWN THE MISSISSIPPI

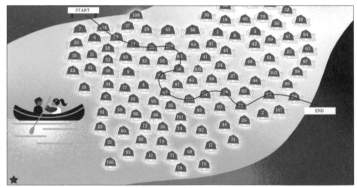

PAGE 49: STAR SHINING BRIGHT

PAGES 52-53: STARS AND STRIPES FOREVER

1. 50
2. 13
3. Red
4. Betsy Ross
5. When someone important has died and from sunrise until noon on Memorial Day.
6. False
7. True
8. June

PAGES 56-57: SAY HELLO!

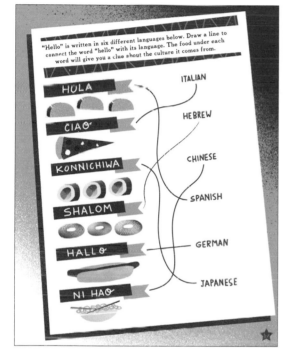

PAGES 58-59: CAMPFIRE CONUNDRUM

There are three pink marshmallows left in the bag.

PAGE 60: GOING SHOPPING

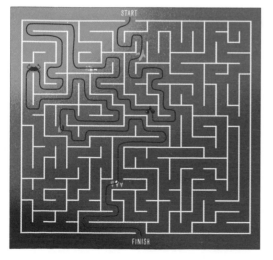

PAGE 61: UNITED SWEETS OF AMERICA

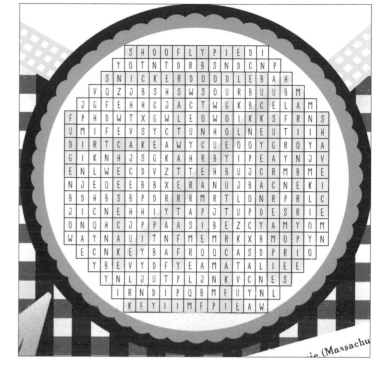

PAGES 64-65: DID I WAKE YOU?

1. 8:00 a.m.

2. 1:00 p.m.

3. 9:00 p.m.

4. 2:00 p.m.

PAGE 66: FLOWER POWER

PAGE 67: ROCKY MOUNTAIN RACE

PAGES 70–71: WACKY & WEIRD

The following three laws are fake:

It's illegal to dance with a coyote in New Mexico.
It's illegal to wear gloves on your feet in Hawai'i.
It's illegal to do a backflip on Thursdays in New Hampshire.

PAGES 72–73: GOLD RUSH!

PAGES 74–75: TICKET TO RIDE

LADORNO = ORLANDO
NAS TONIONA = SAN ANTONIO
OCCIGHA = CHICAGO
HIPHEDALIAPL = PHILADELPHIA
ENW SNOLAER = NEW ORLEANS
ALEEHN = HELENA
NINOLISAMEP = MINNEAPOLIS
VASHLINEL = NASHVILLE

PAGES 76–77: WHO AM I?

 Rosa Parks

 Neil Armstrong

 Thomas Alva Edison

 Benjamin Franklin

 George Washington

Susan B. Anthony

Harriet Tubman

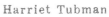

PAGE 80: DERBY DAY

Hamburger
Harp
Hat
Headphones
Heart

Helmet
Hook
Horn
Horseshoe
Hotdog

PAGES 86-87: BEYOND THE USA

1. Buzz Aldrin
2. New Jersey
3. Washington, DC

PAGES 90-91: KNACK FOR NICKNAMES

1. Utah
2. Tennessee
3. Maine
4. Indiana
5. California
6. Wyoming
7. Oregon
8. Texas
9. New Mexico
10. Missouri

PAGES 92-93: THE NATION'S CAPITAL

The following four buildings are not found in Washington, DC:

The Giza Pyramids
Big Ben
Taj Mahal
Eiffel Tower

PAGE 94: HIDE-AND-SEEK

1. Minnesota
2. Idaho
3. Vermont
4. Georgia
5. Arkansas

PAGES 96-97: CRAZY CONTESTS

1. Marshmallow Mash-Up—North Chill, Minnesota
2. The Stink Bug Smell-ebration—Aroma, Delaware
3. Yodel-Off!—Cacophony, Colorado
4. Flame Juggling Fest—Char, Oklahoma
5. Pig Feet Eating Contest—Swineville, Ohio
6. Radish-Eating Contest—Crimson, New Mexico

PAGES 98-99: ALL'S FAIR AT THE STATE FAIR

PAGE 100: DETECTIVE NEEDED

	STATES				PETS			
	Arizona	Florida	Michigan	California	Horse	Fish	Bird	Dog
Kesha		✕			✕			
Laurel	✕						✕	
Marco			✕					✕
Derek				✕	✕			

PAGE 101: FOOTBALL CRISSCROSS

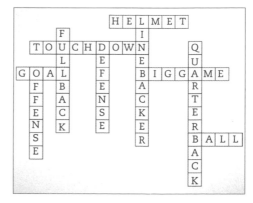

Doodle page

Use this page to draw and
write whatever you like!